The 25 Best Places To Hike With Your Dog In The Ocean State

Doug Gelbert

illustrations by
Andrew Chesworth

Cruden Bay Books

There is always a new trail to look forward to...

DOGGIN' RHODE ISLAND: THE 25 BEST PLACES TO HIKE WITH YOUR DOG IN THE OCEAN STATE

Copyright 2006 by Cruden Bay Books

All rights reserved. No part of this book may be reproduced or transmitted in any form or by any means, electronic or mechanical, including photocopying, recording or by any information storage and retrieval system without permission in writing from the Publisher.

Cruden Bay Books
PO Box 467
Montchanin, DE 19710
www.hikewithyourdog.com

International Standard Book Number 978-0-9795577-2-9

> *"Dogs are our link to paradise...to sit with a dog on a hillside on a glorious afternoon is to be back in Eden, where doing nothing was not boring - it was peace."*
> *- Milan Kundera*

Ahead On The Trail

No Dogs!	12
The 25 Best Places To Hike With Your Dog	15
Taking Your Dog To The Roof Of Rhode Island	66
Your Dog At The Beach	69
Dog Friendly Campgrounds	73
Dog Parks	75
Index To Parks And Open Space	77

Also...

Hiking With Your Dog	5
Outfitting Your Dog For A Hike	7
Low Impact Hiking With Your Dog	10

Introduction

Rhode Island can be a great place to hike with your dog. Within an hour's drive you can hike on sand trails, climb hills that leave your dog panting, walk on some of the most historic grounds in America, explore the estates of America's wealthiest families or circle lakes for miles and never lose sight of the water.

I have selected what I consider to be the 25 best places to take your dog for an outing and ranked them according to subjective criteria including the variety of hikes available, opportunities for canine swimming and pleasure of the walks. The rankings include a mix of parks that feature long walks and parks that contain short walks. Did I miss your favorite? Let us know at *www.hikewithyourdog.com*.

For dog owners it is important to realize that not all parks are open to our best trail companions (see page 12 for a list of parks that do not allow dogs). It is sometimes hard to believe but not everyone loves dogs. We are, in fact, in the minority when compared with our non-dog owning neighbors.

So when visiting a park always keep your dog under control and clean up any messes and we can all expect our great parks to remain open to our dogs. And maybe some others will see the light as well. Remember, every time you go out with your dog you are an ambassador for all dog owners.

So grab that leash and hit the trail!
DBG

Hiking With Your Dog

So you want to start hiking with your dog. Hiking with your dog can be a fascinating way to explore Rhode Island from a canine perspective. Some things to consider:

🐾 Dog's Health

Hiking can be a wonderful preventative for any number of physical and behavioral disorders. One in every three dogs is overweight and running up trails and leaping through streams is great exercise to help keep pounds off. Hiking can also relieve boredom in a dog's routine and calm dogs prone to destructive habits. And hiking with your dog strengthens the overall owner/dog bond.

🐾 Breed of Dog

All dogs enjoy the new scents and sights of a trail. But some dogs are better suited to hiking than others. If you don't as yet have a hiking companion, select a breed that matches your interests. Do you look forward to an entire afternoon's hiking? You'll need a dog bred to keep up with such a pace, such as a retriever or a spaniel. Is a half-hour enough walking for you? It may not be for an energetic dog like a border collie. If you already have a hiking friend, tailor your plans to his abilities.

🐾 Conditioning

Just like humans, dogs need to be acclimated to the task at hand. An inactive dog cannot be expected to bounce from the easy chair in the den to complete a 3-hour hike. You must also be physically able to restrain your dog if confronted with distractions on the trail (like a scampering squirrel or a pack of joggers). Have your dog checked by a veterinarian before significantly increasing your dog's activity level.

🐾 Weather

Hot humid summers do not do dogs any favors. With no sweat glands and only panting available to disperse body heat, dogs are much more susceptible to heat stroke than we are. Unusually rapid panting and/or a bright red tongue are signs of heat exhaustion in your pet.

Always carry enough water for your hike. Even days that don't seem too warm can cause discomfort in dark-coated dogs if the sun is shining brightly. In cold weather, short-coated breeds may require additional attention.

🐾 Trail Hazards

Dogs won't get poison ivy but they can transfer it to you. Stinging nettle is a nuisance plant that lurks on the side of many trails and the slightest brush will deliver troublesome needles into a dog's coat. Some trails are littered with small pieces of broken glass that can slice a dog's paws. Nasty thorns can also blanket trails that we in shoes may never notice.

🐾 Ticks

You won't be able to visit any of Rhode Island's parks without encountering ticks. All are nasty but the deer tick - no bigger than a pin head - carries with it the spectre of Lyme disease. Lyme disease attacks a dog's joints and makes walking painful. The tick needs to be embedded in the skin to transmit Lyme disease. It takes 4-6 hours for a tick to become embedded and another 24-48 hours to transmit Lyme disease bacteria.

When hiking, walk in the middle of trails away from tall grass and bushes. And when the summer sun fades away don't stop thinking about ticks - they remain active any time the temperature is above 30 degrees. By checking your dog - and yourself - thoroughly after each walk you can help avoid Lyme disease. Ticks tend to congregate on your dog's ears, between the toes and around the neck and head.

🐾 Water

Surface water, including fast-flowing streams, is likely to be infested with a microscopic protozoa called *Giardia*, waiting to wreak havoc on a dog's intestinal system. The most common symptom is crippling diarrhea. Algae, pollutants and contaminants can all be in streams, ponds and puddles. If possible, carry fresh water for your dog on the trail - your dog can even learn to drink happily from a squirt bottle.

Outfitting Your Dog For A Hike

These are the basics for taking your dog on a hike:

- **Collar.** It should not be so loose as to come off but you should be able to slide your flat hand under the collar.
- **Identification Tags.** Get one with your veterinarian's phone number as well.
- **Bandanna.** Can help distinguish him from game in hunting season.
- **Leash.** Leather lasts forever but if there's water in your future, consider quick-drying nylon.
- **Water.** Carry 8 ounces for every hour of hiking.

🐾 *I want my dog to help carry water, snacks and other supplies on the trail. Where do I start?*

To select an appropriate dog pack measure your dog's girth around the rib cage. A dog pack should fit securely without hindering the dog's ability to walk normally.

🐾 *Will my dog wear a pack?*

Wearing a dog pack is no more obtrusive than wearing a collar, although some dogs will take to a pack easier than others. Introduce the pack by draping a towel over your dog's back in the house and then having your dog wear an empty pack on short walks. Progressively add some crumpled newspaper and then bits of clothing. Fill the pack with treats and reward your dog from the stash. Soon your dog will associate the dog pack with an outdoor adventure and will eagerly look forward to wearing it.

🐾   *How much weight can I put into a dog pack?*
Many dog packs are sold by weight recommendations. A healthy, well-conditioned dog can comfortably carry 25% to 33% of its body weight. Breeds prone to back problems or hip dysplasia should not wear dog packs. Consult your veterinarian before stuffing the pouches with gear.

🐾   *How does a dog wear a pack?*
The pack, typically with cargo pouches on either side, should ride as close to the shoulders as possible without limiting movement. The straps that hold the dog pack in place should be situated where they will not cause chafing.

🐾   *What are good things to put in a dog pack?*
Low density items such as food and poop bags are good choices. Ice cold bottles of water can cool your dog down on hot days. Don't put anything in a dog pack that can break. Dogs will bang the pack on rocks and trees as they wiggle through tight spots in the trail. Dogs also like to lie down in creeks and other wet spots so seal items in plastic bags. A good use for dog packs when on day hikes around Rhode Island is trail maintenance - your dog can pack out trash left by inconsiderate visitors before you.

🐾 *Are dog booties a good idea?*

Dog booties can be an asset, especially for the occasional canine hiker whose paw pads have not become toughened. Some trails around Rhode Island involve rocky terrain. In some places, there may be broken glass. Hiking boots for dogs are designed to prevent pads from cracking while trotting across rough surfaces. Used in winter, dog booties provide warmth and keep ice balls from forming between toe pads when hiking through snow.

🐾 *What should a doggie first aid kit include?*

Even when taking short hikes it is a good idea to have some basics available for emergencies:
- 4" square gauze pads
- cling type bandaging tapes
- topical wound disinfectant cream
- tweezers
- insect repellent - no reason to leave your dog unprotected against mosquitoes and blackflies
- veterinarian's phone number

I can't think of anything that brings me closer to tears than when my old dog - completely exhausted after a hard day in the field - limps away from her nice spot in front of the fire and comes over to where I'm sitting and puts her head in my lap, a paw over my knee, and closes her eyes, and goes back to sleep. I don't know what I've done to deserve that kind of friend."
-Gene Hill

Low Impact Hiking With Your Dog

Every time you hike with your dog on the trail you are an ambassador for all dog owners. Some people you meet won't believe in your right to take a dog on the trail. Be friendly to all and make the best impression you can by practicing low impact hiking with your dog:

- Pack out everything you pack in.

- Do not leave dog scat on the trail; if you haven't brought plastic bags for poop removal bury it away from the trail and topical water sources.

- Hike only where dogs are allowed.

- Stay on the trail.

- Do not allow your dog to chase wildlife.

- Step off the trail and wait with your dog while horses and other hikers pass.

- Do not allow your dog to bark - people are enjoying the trail for serenity.

- *Have as much fun on your hike as your dog does.*

> "No one appreciates the very special genius of your conversation as a dog does."
> -Christopher Morley

The Other End Of The Leash

Leash laws are like speed limits - everyone seems to have a private interpretation of their validity. Some dog owners never go outside with an unleashed dog; others treat the laws as suggestions or disregard them completely. It is not the purpose of this book to tell dog owners where to go to evade the leash laws or reveal the parks where rangers will look the other way at an unleashed dog. Nor is it the business of this book to preach vigilant adherence to the leash laws. Nothing written in a book is going to change people's behavior with regard to leash laws. So this will be the last time leash laws are mentioned, save occasionally when we point out the parks where dogs are welcomed off leash.

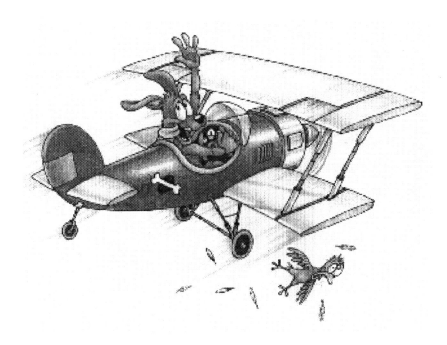

No Dogs

Before we get started on the best places to take your dog, let's get out of the way the trails that do not allow dogs:

Claire D. McIntosh Wildlife Refuge - *Bristol*
Davis Memorial Wildlife Refuge - *North Kingstown*
Emilie Rucker Wildlife Refuge - *Tiverton*
Fisherville Brook Wildlife Refuge - *Exeter*
Florence Sutherland Fort & Richard Knight Fort Wildlife Refuge - *North Smithfield*
George B. Parker Woodland - *Coventry*
John H. Chaffee National Wildlife Refuge - *Narragansett*
Kimball Sanctuary - *Charlestown*
Lathrop Wildlife Refuge - *Westerly*
Lewis-Dickens Farm - *Block Island*

Lime Rock Preserve - *Lincoln*
Long Pond Woods - *Rockville*
Marion Eppley Wildlife Refuge - *West Kingston*
Norman Bird Sanctuary - *Middletown*
Powder Mill Ledges Wildlife Refuge - *Smithfield*
Touisset Marsh Wildlife Refuge - *Warren*
Trustom Pond National Wildlife Refuge - *South Kingstown*
Waterman Pond - *Coventry*

How To Pet A Dog
Tickling tummies slowly and gently works wonders.
Never use a rubbing motion; this makes dogs bad-tempered.
A gentle tickle with the tips of the fingers is all that is necessary
to induce calm in a dog. I hate strangers who go up to dogs with their
hands held to the dog's nose, usually palm towards themselves.
How does the dog know that the hand doesn't hold something horrid?
The palm should always be shown to the dog and go straight
down to between the dog's front legs and tickle gently with
a soothing voice to acompany the action.
Very often the dog raises its back leg in a scratching movement,
it gets so much pleasure from this.
-Barbara Woodhouse

The 25 Best Places To Hike With Your Dog In Rhode Island...

1
Arcadia Management Area

The Park

Arcadia is the largest management area in Rhode Island, keeping almost 14,000 acres in a natural state "more or less," as the state says. Almost the entire area is blanketed in forest cover with a nice mix of leafy deciduous tree and scented white pine.

Elevations range to 541 feet and canine hikers can take advantage of dirt access roads and narrow foot trails, often cushioned by a layer of paw-friendly pine straw.

The Walks

The sheer variety and quality of these shady trails conspire to make Arcadia the best place in Rhode Island for a day of hiking with your dog. Route 165 neatly bisects the forest to use as a starting point for your explorations. There are 30 miles of trails broken into out-and-back segments so you will need to create your own circuit loops or bring two cars for a shuttle to avoid return trips in your own pawprints.

If you want your dog to tackle some of the most rugged hiking in Rhode Island - although it is a stretch to call it strenuous save for the distance - try the *Tippecansett Trail*, the longest trail in the Arcadia system sliced into three equal three-mile legs by two highways. You'll get varied terrain, rocky ledges and swimming ponds on this ramble.

For an exceedingly peaceful hike take the *Ben Utter Trail* north of Route 165 to visit Stepstone Falls. The soft dirt path traces the lively Wood River under giant pines that escaped logging due to their awkward location by the stream and passes foundations of old mills. Another water-enhanced option is the *John B. Hudson Trail* that follows Breakheart Brook to Breakheart Pond.

The *North-South Trail*, a greenway that travels 75 miles for the length of

---

Exeter

Phone Number
- (401) 539-2356

Website
- None

Admission Fee
- None

Directions
- From Interstate 95 take Exit 4. Go three miles north to a blinking yellow light. Go left on Route 165 West and turn left at the sign for the forest office.

> *Bonus*
> If your dog is after views and sniffing in every direction, include the *Mt. Tom Trail* on your agenda. This pleasant trail skirts Parris Brook and climbs quickly but easily to the 430-foot summit - not the highest point in the park but blessed with 360-degree views of miles of treetops from the rocky ledges.

Rhode Island, passes through Arcadia as well. Look for the blue-and-white markers to follow this footpath for awhile.

Trail Sense: There is a trail map that you will want to have in hand before heading out; they are not available at trailheads but can be picked up at the forest headquarters on Arcadia Road. The named trails are not designated at the trailheads and the colored blazes - yellow and white - correspond to trail systems rather than individual trails so you will need to stay alert in your wayfinding.

There is plenty of boulder-hopping for your dog atop Mt. Tom.

Dog Friendliness
Dogs are permitted on the Arcadia trails, campgrounds and in picnic areas but not in swimming areas.

Traffic
Mountain bikers and horses can use the trails but you are likely to go hours without seeing any other trail users on most days. Many dirt roads are gated but others that are not support active vehicular traffic. When hunting season is in progress 200 square inches of blaze orange is required for users of any state management area.

Canine Swimming
There are several ponds to serve as doggie swimming holes and many streams for splashing.

Trail Time
Many hours - or days if you are so inclined.

2
Goddard Memorial State Park

The Park

In the late 1800s Henry Grinnell Russell, like most of his Rhode Island neighbors, walked around a property that was stripped bare by agriculture and deforestation. Russell, who came by this property when he married his Civil War buddy, Captain Thomas P. Ives', sister, wasn't content to lead a treeless life.

As he walked the sandy dunes Russell would drop acorns from his pockets, planting them in holes punched with his cane. He would fill the holes with three acorns - one oak for the squirrels, one for the worms, and one to grow.

Henry Russell would add different trees to his Oaks Estate and by the early 1900s foresters from the U.S. Forest Service called this "the finest example of private forestry in America." After Russell died Colonel Robert Hale Ives Goddard came into possession of the Oaks and continued the reforesting project. When he died in 1927 the estate was left to the state to remain forever in its natural state and opened as a public park on June 1, 1930.

Warwick

Phone Number
- (401) 222-2632

Website
- www.riparks.com/goddard.htm

Admission Fee
- None

Directions
- Goddard Park is on the south side of Greenwich Bay. From Route 1 take Cedar Road east and bear left on Ives Road. Continue past the park exit to the main entrance at 1095 Ives Road.

The Walks

The canine hiking at Goddard Memorial State Park is conducted primarily on bridle paths through the tall forests sandwiched between the bay and the open fields of the picnic areas and golf course. Don't despair about taking your dog down the chewed up paths often associated with horse trails - these wide, sandy avenues through the forest are packed sand and extremely paw-friendly.

This is easy going throughout on gentle terrain. Pick a trail that leads to a dog-friendly beach. At Long Point your dog can indulge in the gentle waves of

> **Bonus**
> The old Oaks estate included many buildings such as barns and the mansion house, which burned down in the 1970s. One structure that survives is the circular wooden building that housed the park's carousel, built in 1931.
> The merry-go-round is gone now but its round enclosure can still be seen near the beach.

Greenwich Cove and you can continue on the sand around to the other side of the main beach. The bridle trail network consists of 18 miles of multi-intersecting short trails.

Trail Sense: The trails are not marked but there is little fear of losing your way. A park map is available, just in case.

Dog Friendliness
Dogs are permitted throughout the park.

Traffic
This is a popular park so expect plenty of company on these trails, including, of course, horses.

Canine Swimming
There is a splendid sand beach on Greenwich Cove around Long Point and plenty of superb dogpaddling in Greenwich Bay.

Trail Time
A half-day of exploring is posible here.

The wide paths at Goddard are a delight for dogs to trot down.

3
The Greenway

The Park

Back in 1972 Block Islanders looked around and noticed houses going up at an alarming rate. Captain John Robinson "Rob" Lewis led a small group to form the Block Island Conservancy with the modest goal to just save Rodman's Hollow, a precious glacial outwash basin. They were able to raise enough money to preserve this region of maritime scrubland.

Hundreds of islanders donated money and the conservation movement flourished. Over the years some land was donated and more made available below market value. Today over 40% of Block Island is protected from future development.

> **Block Island**
>
> Phone Number
> - (401) 466-5675
>
> Website
> - www.nature.org/wherewework/northamerica/states/rhodeisland/preserves/art3146.html
>
> Admission Fee
> - None (ferry fee may be necessary; dogs sail for free)
>
> Directions
> - The Nature Conservancy office on Block Island is on High Street, straight ahead out of Old Harbor.

So effective were the efforts of the Conservancy that the Nature Conservancy designated Block Island as one of its original "Last Great Places" in the Americas.

The Walks

Take away the ferry ride and the half-hour walk along shoulderless - and sometimes busy - two lanes road and The Greenway would be the finest place in Rhode Island to hike with your dog. What is your dog interested in? Open fields? Sporty hills? Long vistas? A romp on the beach? A swim in a pond? Unique woodlands? The Greenway has them all.

There are about 12 miles of footpaths crisscrossing the southern half of Block Island in the tradition of walking the English countryside. In addition to paw-friendly mown grass and soft dirt trails you will need to go down dirt roads and paved streets to get to some trailheads. To reach the beach use Black Rock

> **_Bonus_**
> Block Island supports some 40 rare or endangered species. One that is found only in Rodman's Hollow, in huge kettleholes gouged by Godzilla-sized chunks of glacial ice that melted, is the Block Island Meadow Vole, first discovered in 1908. It is part of the magic of the island that it is a thrill here to see rodents considered vermin on the mainland. It's not easy to see a brown-and-black vole but you may see their tunnel-like trails through the grass.

Road in Rodman's Hollow. If you find yourself with your dog walking along Mohegan Trail/Spring Street you can descend a flight of wooden stairs to the beach at the foot of the spectacular Mohegan bluffs from Payne Overlook.

Trail Sense: Your first stop on Block Island should be in the Visitor Center on the dock to buy a trail map for a small fee. This will show you the way to the trailheads. Signs are posted at some trailheads and along the trails.

Dog Friendliness
Block Island is a dog-friendly island - don't come without him!
Traffic
As magnificent as they are, the walking paths are your best place to find tranquility on the island; dirt roads allow bikes but not mopeds.
Canine Swimming
There are 17 miles of public beaches on Block Island so your dog will get an ocean swim. Crescent Beach, a few pawprints from the ferry landing, is the most convenient but crowded in-season. As the new arrivals fan out from the ferry the beaches offer more room for your dog. One beach that is too small for sun worshippers but ideal for dogs is just south of Old Harbor along Spring Street - as you reach the crest of a hill drop down to the sand in front of a guardrail for great canine swimming along a breakwater.
Trail Time
Allow a full day of canine hiking to explore The Greenway.

Sometimes it seems like nature made the beach at Mohegan Bluffs just for dogs.

4
Beavertail State Park

The Park

The first lighthouse built at Beavertail was the third in the country when it was constructed in 1749 - after only the Boston Harbor Light (1716) and the Great Point Light on Nantucket (1746). Four years later the Newport Light, as it was called, became America's first lighthouse to burn to the ground.

The rubble tower that was built next lasted a full century until it was replaced by the current granite tower that guides vessels into Narragansett Bay today.

The United States Navy took control of this point in World War II and erected Fort Burnside in honor of Civil War general and Rhode Island governor Ambrose Burnside. In 1980 the state acquired the land as surplus property.

Jamestown

Phone Number
- (401) 423-9941

Website
- www.riparks.com/beaverta1.htm

Admission Fee
- None

Directions
- From Route 138 exit towards the town of Jamestown on North Main Road. Continue to South East Avenue and pick up Beavertail Road to the end.

The Walks

Canine hikers can come to Beavertail for the Cliff Walk without the tourists - especially in the off-season. You can hike with your dog from one end of the park to the other atop the rocky shoreline on park roads and a narrow dirt path. If the weather is calm and the seas benign you can include the craggy rocks in your route.

The views will be spectacular at almost any point in your hike with four specific overlooks designated. Interpretive signs describe the area, including the Beavertail fault with its geologic story of ancient Rhode Island.

Make sure to bring plenty of fresh water for your dog at Beavertail. There isn't much shade out on the point and no drinking water.

Trail Sense: There are no marked trails or map but nowhere to get lost.

> *Bonus*
> The Beavertail Light celebrates its 150th year of operation in 2006 at the southern end of Conanicut Island. In addition to the lighthouse and a museum there is a small aquarium in an old fog horn building where you can see creatures from the tidal pools in the rocks below.

A trail option at Beavertail State Park takes your dog down on the rocks around the historic lighthouse that has stood since 1856.

Dog Friendliness
Dogs are welcome throughout Beavertail State Park.
Traffic
On any nice day there will be plenty of folks picking their way along the slabs of broken rock.
Canine Swimming
If the waters are calm your dog can catch a swim in a tidal pool but you don't want her to get too adventurous.
Trail Time
Without sightseeing, there is less than an hour of hiking here.

5
Clay Head Nature Trail

The Park

David and Elise Lapham first visited Block Island for a vacation in 1951. Over the next decade they kept returning and finally decided to buy five acres on the island's north end. While looking at a small parcel of land across the road they ended up instead with almost 200 acres atop the clay bluffs gouged out by retreating glaciers some 10,000 years prior.

David Lapham discovered he had an affinity for trail building. He picked up a chopping machine and began clawing out brush and thickets in every direction. One day he set out to measure his walking paths and found out he had nine miles of trails on his property.

Block Island
Phone Number - (401) 466-5675
Website - www.nature.org/wherewework/northamerica/states/rhodeisland/preserves/art3146.html
Admission Fee - None (ferry fee may be necessary; dogs sail for free)
Directions - From Old Harbor, head north on the Corn Neck Road (the only road to the north end of Block Island) to the trailhead at a post marker about 2.5 miles from town.

With his trail system complete the Lathams began decorating the footpaths. Over the years more than 7,000 daffodil bulbs went into the ground. Thousands of trees were planted. From the beginning, the Laphams wanted to share their land with its spectacular setting. When they decided to leave the property in the stewardship of the Nature Conservancy it was with the proviso that the public would have access to the trails.

The Walks

David Lapham's trail system has come to be known as "The Maze." These grassy trails are unmarked but well-maintained and a delight for your dog. You can pop out at a stone wall or one of the best views on the East Coast. The *Clay Head Nature Trail* runs for about one mile along the top of the 70-foot bluffs. It is easy going but will be one of the longest miles you've ever taken your

> *Bonus*
> Setting out from the northern terminus of the Clay Head Trail you can reach the North Light with your dog after about a 20-minute walk on a sandy beach. Dangerous shoals and frequent fog banks made the passage around Block Island a tricky affair for mariners. Between 1819 and 1839 alone fifty-nine ships wrecked on or near Block Island.
> The current granite lighthouse dates to 1868 and was the fourth light to be built here. The first three, dating to 1829, fell victim to shifting sands, faulty design and voracious waves.

dog on when you factor in the frequent stops for watching the crashing waves or chartng the progress of a passing vessel.

Trail Sense: Your first stop on Block Island should be in the Visitor Center on the dock to buy a trail map for a small fee. This will show you the way to the trailheads. Signs are posted at some trailheads and along the trails.

Dog Friendliness
Dogs are allowed on the Clay Head Trail. The North Light is on land managed by the Block Island National Wildlife Refuge that is the only one of Rhode Island's five national refuges that allow dogs but that could change.

Traffic
This is one of the prime destinations on Block Island but there is plenty of trail space to spread out. Foot traffic only.

Canine Swimming
Take a trail to the beach and let your dog enjoy the waves.

Trail Time
If you have to make the walk from the ferry up Corn Neck Road to the trailhead this canine hike will last at least half the day, depending on how much time you devote to The Maze, the beach or the views.

6
George Washington Management Area

The Park

In the Spring of 1965 over 300 Australian sailors were in the United States awaiting delivery on their guided missile destroyer, the *HMAS Perth*, that was being readied in Bay City, Michigan. The original *HMAS Perth* had been torpedoed in World War II at the Battle of Sunda Strait and sank with the loss of 350 of her crew and three civilians. Another 324 of the Perth's crew survived the sinking and were taken prisoner.

Glocester
Phone Number - (401) 568-2013
Website - None
Admission Fee - None
Directions - The management area is in northwestern Rhode Island on Route 44, two miles east of the Connecticut border.

With six weeks down time ahead of them the problem arose of how to keep the men occupied. The Division of Forests in Rhode Island had a solution: come and help develop the George Washington Forest. So work groups of 100 Aussie sailors rotated on two-week tours in the Rhode Island wilderness felling trees, building picnic areas and carving trails.

By all accounts the sailors had a splendid time with their enforced shore leave. They worked hard and played hard, enjoying swimming in the adjacent Bowdish Reservoir. Visitors have been enjoying their efforts ever since.

After her commission on July 17, 1965 the *HMAS Perth* was deployed in Vietnam and came under fire four times. It was the only Australian ship to be hit by enemy fire and was awarded the United States Navy Meritorious Unit Commendation for her service. On November 24, 2001 the *HMAS Perth* was sunk as a dive wreck off the Western Australian coast.

The Walks

The *Walkabout Trail* contructed by the Australians is a six-mile loop with several cut-offs to shorten the canine hike. They appear to have done a superior job in scouting the peripatetic route for as you walk along the trail seems to pass

> **_Bonus_**
> You can scarcely find a more enchanting invitation to hike with your dog than at the Walkabout Trail: "The Australian aborigine occasionally reverts to his Stone Age state and follows an impulsive urge to wander through the bush with his family. This urge to wander is called 'going walkabout' and the places visited are usually connected with his tribal spirits of land and air from the 'Dreamtime.' We invite you to go walkabout on this trail of this beautiful countryside."

through the prettiest scenery on the property. Those surroundings include rock outcroppings, marshlands, a white Cedar swamp and a grove of dark, Eastern hemlocks. This is easy going for any dog with small hillocks and a well-maintained path.

There are many other trails that lead off the Walkabout, including a spur to Peck Pond to expand your dog's day in the Geroge Washington Memorial State Forest but you will still cover but a fraction of its more than 3,000 acres.

Trail Sense: The Walkabout Trail is enthusiastically blazed and a trail map is available at the forest office.

Dog Friendliness
Dogs are welcome on the trails, campgrounds and in picnic areas but not on the swimming beach.

Traffic
Dirt bikes and the occasional vehicle on the sand roads are normally a minor concern.

Canine Swimming
The Walkabout Trail touches briefly on Bowdish Reservoir and spends more time at Wilbur Pond for canine refreshment.

Trail Time
Several hours to a full day.

If there are no dogs in Heaven,
then when I die I want to go where they went.
-Anonymous

7
Cliff Walk

The Park

In the late 1800s wealthy New Yorkers began coming to Newport to escape the suffocating summer heat in the city. They built the most extravagant "cottages" ever seen in America on the rocky bluffs overlooking the Atlantic Ocean.

No matter how impressive the mansion or how rich the owner, however, no one's property could extend all the way to the shoreline. By virtue of "Fisherman's Rights" granted by the Colonial Charter of King Charles II and a provision in the Rhode Island Constitution, the public is always guaranteed the legal right to walk along a small sliver of cliff.

Newport

Phone Number
- None

Website
- www.cliffwalk.com

Admission Fee
- None

Directions
- The Cliff Walk begins at Memorial Boulevard and ends at the southern end of Bellevue Avenue. In the off-season there may be parking near the northern terminus at First Beach.

Not that the powerful residents on the other sides of the gates have always agreed with that right. In the past bushes were planted, walls erected and even bulls grazed to discourage use by the public. Other owners embraced the Cliff Walk and helped develop it from a mere footpath. Some tunnels were built and flagstones placed in muddy stretches. Eventually the federal government stepped in to help rebuild the path after erosion during hurricanes. In 1975, the Cliff Walk was named the first National Recreation Trail in New England.

The Walks

Today the *Cliff Walk* rambles for about 3.5 miles, about two of which are paved and easy to hike. The first mile calls to mind a stroll in a city park with manicured grass and an abundance of flowers. Your dog will be walking on nail-grinding asphalt and concrete sidewalk.

As you move along the path deteriorates into broken asphalt and dirt but

> **Bonus**
> Adjacent to the northern end of the Cliff Walk is First Beach, open to dogs in the off-season. There is about 3/4 of a mile of sandy shoreline to hike with your dog here. Also at the beach is the New England Exploration Center with a hands-on touch tank and 1950s-era carousel.

the views improve as you reach the jawdropping relics of the Gilded Age - mansions constructed as summer cottages from about 1870 to 1915.

Continuing past the paved path, the Cliff Walk turns rustic with some walking on unprotected, open cliff faces and boulder hopping. It requires concentration but any level of canine hiker can negotiate the trip. If you continue to the end of the Cliff Walk you will drop to ocean's edge and Reject's Beach where your dog can get a swim. At the end of the Cliff Walk you have the option of returning by the same route along the black Atlantic rocks or exiting into the town and walking back on the sidewalks in front of the mansions whose backyards you have just walked through.

Trail Sense: None needed.

Dog Friendliness
Dogs are welcome all along the Cliff Walk and Poop Bags are even provided at the start on Memorial Boulevard.

Traffic
Foot traffic only and extremely crowded anytime the weather is good. After the short tunnel at Sheep's Point when the boulders start the traffic thins appreciably.

Canine Swimming
If the sea is agreeable there is the opportunity for an ocean swim.

Trail Time
The full canine hike back to your start point will last about three hours.

> *"Any man who does not like dogs and want them does not deserve to be in the White House."*
> *-Calvin Coolidge*

8
Weetamoo Woods

The Park

This land was originally part of the Massachusetts Bay Colony, known as Pocasset and home to the Wamponoag-Pocasset tribe. The Wamponoag-Pocassets were the Indians of Pilgrim fame who helped the English settlers survive the harsh early days and participated in the first Thanksgiving dinner.

Things were not so civil a half-century later when the warrior Metacom, given the English name Philip by his tribal chief father, led a rebellion against the British. He was aided in his cause by his widowed sister-in-law, Weetamoo, that translates to "sweetheart."

During the King Philip War in the summer of 1675 Metacom and Weetamoo used the swamp here to hideout from British patrols. They might well have succeded in defeating the British were it not for rival tribes in the region and on August 12, 1676 King Philip was killed and the remnants of his tribe dispersed or sold into slavery.

The 450 acres of woodlands was acquired by the town of Tiverton in 1990.

Tiverton Four Corners

Phone Number
- None

Website
- None

Admission Fee
- None

Directions
- The park is bordered by Main Road (Route 77) to the west and Lake Road to the east, north of Tiverton Four Corners. Traveling south from Tiverton on Route 77, make a left on East Road (Route 179) in town. The main kiosk is on the left. There are also small parking lots on Lake Road and Lafayette Road (north side of the property).

The Walks

The best canine hiking in Weetamoo Woods is along the *Red Trail* that travels part of the way on the Eight Rod Way, surveyed in 1679 as a road between Sakonnet and Plymouth Colony. Today the old road is ideal for your dog to trot along through one of the last large, unfragmented forested areas along the New England coast. Look for American holly trees in the understory of this unusual oak-holly forest.

> **_Bonus_**
> Along the Red Trail you will find the remains of the Borden sawmill that dates back to Revolutionary times. Further exploration nearby will reveal the ruins of mill worker's homes - foundations and cellar holes. Blocks of stone were used to create the mill race along Borden Brook and the rare stone arch and slab bridges over the stream.

The Red Trail connects to the *Yellow Trail* that runs down the spine of the property. Don't neglect the short connecting spurs that lead to the regenerating Atlantic cedar swamp (*Green Trail*) and the 170-foot High Rock (*Blue Trail*). These short routes can be used to create hiking loops with the two main trails, each a bit over a mile long.

Trail Sense: The trails are well blazed but there may not be any maps available at the trailhead. The Yellow Trail runs between East Road and Lafayette Road and the Red Trail leads to Lake Road.

Dog Friendliness
Dogs are welcome in Weetamoo Woods.
Traffic
The old roads attract mountain bikers and the easy terrain is a lure for joggers but competition for the trails is scarcely overwhelming.
Canine Swimming
Borden Brook is good for a refreshing splash but not a doggie swim.
Trail Time
The entire trail system can be covered in about two hours.

9
Heritage Park

The Park
The town of Glocester has preserved former farmland into 127 acres of open space.

The Walks
The trail system stretches for nearly two miles on stacked loops, completely under the shaded canopy of an emerging forest. In an unusual switch, your dog will probably prefer the multi-use trail to the footpath at Heritage Park. It is a wide and wonderful canine hike on wood chips that rolls past rock outcroppings and across streams.

The yellow footpath, although it trips merrily along an energetic stream, grows constricting along much of its route. Use it to extend your trip through this airy forest but don't make it your first destination.

Trail Sense: There is a painted mapboard to consult at the trailhead. The trails are not blazed but marked by signs at junctions - some placed curiously high in the trees so look up as you come to a trail fork or you might miss them.

Glocester

Phone Number
- None

Website
- None

Admission Fee
- None

Directions
- The park is located off Putnam Pike (Route 44) between Harmony and Chepachet. Heading west, turn left onto Chestnut Oak Road at a bend in the main road. The park is less than one mile on the left.

Dog Friendliness
Dogs are welcome on these walking paths.
Traffic
Mountain bikers and hikers find their way to Heritage Park to join the dog walkers.
Canine Swimming
The stream is suited only for fish swimming.
Trail Time
About one hour.

Bonus

After your hike toddle up the road to the village of Chepachet and show your dog the spot on the bridge over the Chepachet River where Betty, the Learned Elephant, was shot and killed on May 25, 1826.

Little Bett was the second Indian elephant on North American shores, owned by Hakaliah Bailey.

Bailey's first elephant, Big Bett, arrived in 1796 and he traveled the East Coast displaying the pachyderm until it was shot by a Maine farmer in 1816.

Five years later Little Bett arrived as a replacement and her career was cut short prematurely when she met the same fate on the old wooden bridge.

The incident caused purveyors of traveling exotic animal shows to seek a more respectable image and led directly to the formation of the American circus.

A reconstructed sheep herder's hut along the trail in Heritage Park can provide welcome shade for a dog on a during a hot day of hiking.

10
Buck Hill Management Area

The Park
This parcel of 2000+ acres fits nicely into the far northwestern corner of the state, bounded by Connecticut and Massachusetts. The state has actively managed the land, transforming the former farmland into a vast woodland with wetlands created to attract wildlife.

The Walks
The premier hike in the Buck Hill Management Area is a loop of just under five miles using the yellow and white trails - an ideal distance to cover before your dog starts getting bored. The entire preserve is virtually under deciduous tree cover making this an excellent autumn choice for a canine hike.

This is easy going for any dog on dirt roads and well-marked trails. Along the way you will pass into Connecticut and Massachusetts and hopefully spy the tri-state marker.

Trail Sense: The trails are marked but a map may be hard to come by.

Burrillville

Phone Number
- (401) 222-2632

Website
- None

Admission Fee
- None

Directions
- Follow Route 100 North (Wallum Lake Road) to Buck Hill Road on the left. The entrance is 2.3 miles down after the turnoff.

Dog Friendliness
Dogs are welcome to join the fun at Buck Hill.

Traffic
The main trail is hiker-only. When hunting season is in progress 200 square inches of blaze orange is required for users of any state management area.

Canine Swimming
If your travels bring you to Wallum Lake your dog can get superb dog paddling in at a boat ramp.

Trail Time
Several hours.

> **Bonus**
> When you come to the marsh you will see hundreds of ghost trees, killed when a dike was built to create the marsh. These skeleton trees - dead, still standing but not decomposed - are common sights in ocean dunesland but can be startling in an otherwise vibrant forestscape.

To err is human, to forgive, canine.
-Anonymous

11
Prudence Island

The Park

Prudence Island, in the geographic center of Narragansett Bay, was a possession of the Narragansett tribe, known as Chibchuwesa - "a place apart." Roger Williams purchased Prudence, Hope and Patience islands, so named by the state founder for three virtues everyone should possess.

Settlement came slowly and those who came to the island farmed exclusively until the early 1900s. In 1921 Halsey Chase started a ferry service from Bristol to help fill the guest rooms in his island hotel. Summer cottages sprang up along the shoreline as well.

The resort life was interrupted during World War II when the U.S. Navy built a munitions base and the Army established an army camp. The Navy kept its base until 1972. In 1980 much of Prudence Island and all of Hope and Patience islands were designated the Narragansett Bay National Estuarine Research Reserve.

Mercer

Phone Number
- (401) 253-9808 (ferry)

Website
- None

Admission Fee
- None (ferry ticket)

Directions
- The Prudence Island Ferry is at Church Street Wharf in Bristol.

The Walks

Any visit with your dog to Prudence Island will be on foot, disembarking from the ferry. A network of walking trails and uncrowded roads visit the island's unique habitats, including a region of pine barrens at the south end of the island. The extremely dry, dunes-like soil makes up just 4 of every 1000 acres of land mass in Rhode Island.

There are plenty of paw-friendly mown grass trails for your dog to sample through the woods and meadows. Try to keep your dog as centered as possible in the natural areas since Prudence Island supports the densest herd of whitetail deer in New England. Be even more fastidious than usual checking your dog for ticks after canine hiking on the island.

> *Bonus*
> The Research Reserve created an acclaimed
> butterfly garden on the island in 1997,
> using such native species as joe-pye weed,
> pink tickseed, and lupine and to enhance the habitat
> for many of Prudence Island's rare butterfly species.
> Island elementary students planted 20 trumpet
> vine plants and made stepping stones as they learned
> about pesticide-free insect control.

Unlike Block Island, there are no great "must-see" destinations on Prudence Island. Prudence Island is a place for a relaxed pace for your dog to trot along.

Trail Sense: There isn't always a sign for the trails but you should be able to navigate your way around the island.

Dog Friendliness
Dogs are allowed on the ferry and the island.
Traffic
Practically none, especially in the off-season.
Canine Swimming
Sandy beaches are not the norm on Prudence Island but your dog can find a swim in calm waters.
Trail Time
Allow a day to fully explore the island on foot.

Brenton Point State Park

The Park

William Brenton was in his early 30s when he sailed for Boston from England in 1633. In 1637 he was part of the founding band of settlers of Newport. He became Deputy Governor of the towns of Portsmouth and Newport and took possession of some 2000 acres here in 1639. He named it "Hammersmith" after his home in England.

Two centuries after the governor's death in 1674 the property was acquired by Theodore M. Davis, a lawyer and famous Egyptologist. He built a large shingled mansion overlooking the sea called "the Reef" that became one of the most distinctive residences in Newport, characterized by beautiful formal gardens.

The Reef fell victim to messy divorces and World War II when the United States Army took over the estate and used it as a sight for a Coastal Artillery Battery. Following the war the mansion was never re-occupied and after years of vandalism eventually burned and was razed. In 1969 the State of Rhode Island took over the property and opened Brenton Point State Park in 1976.

Newport

Phone Number
- (401) 849-4562 (in season)

Website
- www.riparks.com/brenton.htm

Admission Fee
- None

Directions
- The park is on Ocean Drive. Take Route 114 South (West Main Road) to 138 South to Broadway in downtown Newport. Follow the signs to Ocean Drive.

The Walks

Your canine hiking day at Brenton Point is left to your imagination. There is a paved one-mile oceanfront walking path or you can explore the ruins of the old estate on access roads and wide grass paths. The debris from the Reef is buried under the mound overlooking the Atlantic but still standing are the remains of an elaborate L-shaped stable and a stone tower that your dog can climb to a viewing stand.

> *Bonus*
> The grassy oceanside expanses at Brenton Point are not merely an awesome setting for a game of fetch but a mecca for kiteflying enthusiasts.
> In July the Newport Kite Festival brings together elaborate kites from all over the world to fly on the former grounds of the Reef.

This is an easy go for any dog although the trails through the reeds at the back of the property can be a tight squeeze if attempted.

Based on the places dogs are allowed to hike in Rhode Island it should be called the "Forest State" so this open-air outing for your dog is a real treat.

Trail Sense: There is no map and nothing is marked but none is needed.

Your dog can clamber up the steps to the top of an old stone tower and soak in views of the Atlantic Ocean and the ruins of the once-spectacular stables.

Dog Friendliness
This is the place to come for dogs to get the feel of the grounds of the fabled Newport estates.

Traffic
Off-season is best.

Canine Swimming
This is not the place to test the roiling waves of the Atlantic.

Trail Time
A leisurely hour.

Happiness is dog-shaped.
-Chapman Pincher

13
Fort Barton Nature Walk

The Park

The British occupation of Newport in December 1776 inspired the Tiverton Heights fortifications of July 1777. Its first commander, for whom the fort was subsequently named, was Lieutenant Colonel William Barton.

In just his first week of command, Barton successfully led a raiding party of 40 men across Mount Hope Bay to kidnap occupation commander General Richard Preston in his bedroom in Middletown. Barton was hailed as a hero and celebrated for his boldness. The Americans had received the morale boost they were longing for.

Later Fort Barton was the launching point for General John Sullivan's invasion force during the muddled Battle of Rhode Island. In a bizarre postscript, William Barton was remanded to debtor's prison for 14 years for refusing to pay a judgement on Vermont land he had purchased. When the Marquis de Lafayette, who coordinated the French naval forces in the Battle of Rhode Island, visited the United States in 1824 he discovered Barton in prison and paid the claim.

Tiverton
Phone Number - None
Website - None
Admission Fee - None
Directions - From Route 138, take Route 77 south to Lawton Avenue. Turn left and follow Lawton two blocks to its end at Highland Road. The park is directly ahead on top of the hill; parking is available at the base of the hill.

The Walks

Behind the grassy redoubt of Fort Barton a flight of steep wooden steps drop down into 80 acres of lush woodlands. Here are some three miles of sporty canine hiking that explore ravines and streambeds. The main route is along the *Red Trail* that makes a large buttonhook out and around a hill of boulders. The Red Trail is intertwined at several junctions by the *Blue Trail* that twists around it. Staircases and log bridges smooth out the rougher edges of this ramble.

> **Bonus**
> Sitting on the site of Fort Barton is a
> 30-foot observation tower that affords superb views
> of Mount Hope Bay and the Sakonnet River.
> Your dog can easily climb the wide steps and
> enjoy the westward views as well.

The centerpiece of the property is Sin and Flesh Brook, whose name derives from a grisly incident on March 28, 1676. Zoeth Howland, apparently a devout sort, was riding from Dartmouth to Newport to attend a Quaker meeting. He was following this very stream in Tiverton when he was ambushed by six Indians who killed Howland and left his corpse into the stream. When his body was discovered the brook got its name.

Trail Sense: The trails are well-marked and a trail map is available at Tiverton town hall.

Dog Friendliness
Dogs are allowed to hike the Fort Barton ravines.
Traffic
Foot traffic only and generally quiet.
Canine Swimming
Most dogs will not find the Flesh and Sin Brook deep enough for swimming.
Trail Time
Expect to spend about an hour on these trails.

14
Burlingame State Park

The Park

After World War I Americans fully embraced a love affair with the automobile that has never abated. Road construction exploded and the American people began heading for the great outdoors like never before. The result was the first National Conference on Outdoor Recreation, sponsored by the White House, in 1925.

Out of this conference grew Burlingame Reservation with land purchased between 1927 and 1934. The park was named for Edwin Alysworth Burlingame who was the chairman of Rhode Island's Metropolitan Park Commission at the time.

The centerpiece of Burlingame's more than 3,000 acres is the 573-acre natural Watchaug Pond. The waters, with an average depth of only eight feet, are a hotspot for bass fishermen and a magnet for kayakers and canoeists.

Charlestown

Phone Number
- (401) 322-8910

Website
- www.riparks.com/burlinga.htm

Admission Fee
- None

Directions
- Take Interstate 95 South to Route 4 South to Route 1 South into Charlestown. Turn at the Burlingame Picnic Area Sign.

> **_Bonus_**
> Burlingame has been synonymous with camping for Rhode Islanders for more than half-a-century. During the Great Depression, the reservation was the headquarters of Burlingame Camp, 141st Company, Civilian Conservation Corps (CCC), the first CCC camp in the state. Millions of men were put to work by President Franklin Roosevelt in rural areas building roads, working on flood control and beautification projects. During World War II several units of the Yankee Division, which did beach patrol, were stationed here. The old CCC buildings are still in use for youth camps today.

The Walks

The star walk at Burlingame is the 7.9-mile *Vin Gormley Trail* that circumnavigates the pond. Once you are in for a penny on this canine hike you are in for a pound since the only shortcut available is by boat, unless you choose to retrace your steps. Much of the way will be across rocky terrain and through pine forests (the official Rhode Island Christmas tree was harvested in Burlingame for years) and there is an inconvenient stretch of some two miles where you need to take your dog along narrow two-lane roads. To complete the entire yellow-blazed loop will take about four hours.

Trail Sense: A trail map is available and it breaks the Vin Gormley loop into timed segments for those who don't want to take on the entire hike.

Dog Friendliness
Dogs are not allowed in the public beach area.
Traffic
Cyclists can try these trails and the uneven terrain even hosts races for runners such as the annual Lil' Thody Runaround.
Canine Swimming
Just try and keep your dog out of Watchaug Pond.
Trail Time
Many hours of trail time here.

15

Fort Wetherill State Park

The Park

For most of its time in American history these high granite bluffs looking down on the East Passage of Narragansett Bay has led a military life, albeit deactivated for the most part. Colonists built an earthern battery here and when it was known as Dumpling Rock the United States built Fort Dumpling in the early 1800s.

As coastal defenses ratcheted up around 1900 the fortifications were beefed up and the fort was renamed in honor of Captain Alexander Wetherill, a local infantryman killed in the Battle of San Juan during the Spanish American War.

During World War II the old fort saw its last active duty - as a training center. It closed in 1946; it's guns hidden in the cliffs never used. In 1972 the State of Rhode Island acquired the property for a park.

Jamestown

Phone Number
- (401) 423-1771

Website
- www.riparks.com/fortweth.htm

Admission Fee
- None

Directions
- The park is on the east side of Conanicut Island. From Route 138 travel to and through Jamestown to Canonicus Avenue. Take Walcott Avenue to Fort Wetherill Road and the park.

The Walks

The canine hiking at Fort Wetherill is mostly on narrow dirt trails out to rocky promontories overlooking the sea. What they lack in distance they more than make up for in aesthetic appeal. At land's end the short hike is to the remains of the old battery.

The only marked trail is a *Nature Trail* but don't get excited - it only goes up and down a small hill between parking lots. Don't neglect it, however, for its views are riveting.

Trail Sense: Nothing is available to lead you around the 60-acre park. Park at the first of the three parking lots and make your way to land's end.

> *Bonus*
> A spur up the hill from the Nature Trail leads to a concealed battery built in the hillside. The guns at Batteries Wheaton and Varnum in Fort Wetherill could launch 1,000-pound shells at a target for over six miles.

Dog Friendliness
Dogs are free to use the Fort Wetherill trails.
Traffic
Little; foot traffic only on the trails.
Canine Swimming
Some of the best canine swimming in Rhode Island is available in the cove below the middle parking lot.
Trail Time
Less than one hour.

In the coves at Fort Wetherill can be found some of the best dog paddling in Rhode Island and are the main reason to bring your dog here.

16
Cumberland Monastery

The Park

1825 Dom Vincent founded the modest Abbey of Petit Clairvaux in Tracadie, Nova Scotia. The order remained productive until 1892 when a fire destroyed the abbey.

Seeking a new home for the Monastery of Our Lady of the Strict Observance, Dom John Murphy found 530 acres of land in Cumberland in August of 1900. The monks quarried stone on the property to build the new Abbey of Our Lady of the Valley and cleared the fields. The monastery was completely self-sufficient with a community of over 100 monks.

Cumberland
Phone Number - None
Website - None
Admission Fee - None
Directions - The trail system is accessible behind the Cumberland Library at 1464 Diamond Hill Road (Route 114) in town.

In 1950 another fire struck. It took 10 fire companies to bring the conflagration under control. No one was killed but the cost to rebuild was estimated at two million 1950 dollars. The order moved instead to Spencer, Massachusetts.

The town of Cumberland now owns the property and the public library rests on the site of the former Cistercian monastery.

The Walks

The main drag at the Cumberland Monastery is a rambling crushed gravel path that slips in and out of the wooded hillsides. One stretch in the back of the park ambles through open spaces that is actually one of the few open air hikes you can take with your dog away from the coastline. The open area could come in handy if confronted with a phantom horse rider that is said to "come upon you out of nowhere" from the woods. Other tales of haunted trails at the Monastery report of the ghost of a child running near the swamp area on the back trails. Pay attention if your dog's ears perk up for no apparent reason here.

The paths are wide and the understory light that gives these paths a big

> *Bonus*
> King Philip's War (1675-76) is one of the most overlooked, yet bloody, conflicts to have occurred on American soil. In the battle between colonists and Native Americans in New England one in ten soldiers on both sides was wounded or killed. The English were almost pushed back to the shoreline. One of their worst defeats came on Sunday morning March 26, 1676, when Captain Michael Pierce and a company of 63 English and 20 friendly Wampanoag Indians was ambushed in a ravine near Attleborough Gore on the Blackstone River by about 500 Narragansett led by chief sachem Canonchet. Most of the Colonists, including Pierce, were killed.
> Nine Englishmen were taken to a spot on this property where they were tortured and killed.
> The mens' remains were buried by settlers in a spot marked by a boulder monument to Nine Men's Misery.

feel. Other trails run to the edges of the property that stretch the trail system here to several miles.

Trail Sense: None, just jump on the trails and start hiking.

Dog Friendliness

There are so many dog walkers at the Monastery it almost seems to be a requirement.

Traffic

Foot traffic but the paths are wide.

Canine Swimming

There are two small ponds on the property that may be clean enough for a dog swim.

Trail Time

About one hour.

17
Lincoln Woods State Park

The Park

In 1820, when most Americans were busy cutting down trees and clearing land for farms and roads and towns, Zacariah Allen had another idea. He thought that "vacant land may profitably be improved by planting to trees." He was only 25 at the time.

He set about planting scores of American chestnuts and oaks on farmlands and pasture in this area exhausted from use for over 100 years. It was the first documented attempt at silviculture - the science, art and practice of caring for forests with respect to human objectives -in the United States.

Lincoln
Phone Number - (401) 723-7892
Website - www.riparks.com/lincoln.htm
Admission Fee - None
Directions - From Interstate 5 take Exit 23 to Route 146 North to park.

Allen pulled profits from his tree business for 57 years. Later his descendents sold his land to the State of Rhode Island for $1,800 in what would become the new Lincoln Woods Reservation. The first 70 acres for the park was acquired by the Metropolitan Park System in 1908. A year later, on February 12, the Centennial of Abraham Lincoln's birthday, the park was dedicated in the name of the 16th President. Today's park encompasses 627 acres.

The Walks

There are no specific destinations in store for a canine outing here - just a chance to get out in the woods and hike. There are close to a dozen miles of dirt scars through the hillsides for you to try. There are no prescribed routes through the trees and around the boulders. Expect a vigorous workout for your dog on the Lincoln Woods trails, especially if you go for miles. Bring plenty of fresh water on hot days since you will be working away from Olney Pond.

Trail Sense: The trails are not marked and not blazed. Your dog should come with a nose to explore.

> *Bonus*
> Lincoln Woods is among the top areas in New England for bouldering. While on the trail you can watch practicioners working on their techniques on the smooth granite boulders. Or try it yourself. The best time to boulder at Lincoln Woods is in the fall or early winter.

Dog Friendliness
Dogs are welcome in the park but not in the swimming areas.
Traffic
A popular mountain biking spot and horses use the trails as well. In good weather expect great competition for the trails.
Canine Swimming
Find a spot around Olney Lake and toss a stick in for yor dog.
Trail Time
Many hours.

18
Colt State Park

The Park

Samuel Colt, whose uncle developed the revolver that won the West, was a New Jersey native who spent much time in his mother's hometown of Bristol growing up. After graduating from Columbia Law School he returned to Bristol to make it his home.

In 1887 he organized the Industrial Trust Company bank and later took control of the bankrupt hometown India Rubber Company. He transformed the floundering enterprise into the U.S. Rubber Company, becoming the dominant producer in the industry.

Bristol
Phone Number - (908) 638-6969
Website - www.riparks.com/colt.htm
Admission Fee - None
Directions - The park is west of Bristol on Route 114.

In Bristol he purchased several old family farms on Poppasquash Neck to create Colt Farm that he conceived as a beauty spot for the public to enjoy. He engraved an open invitation on the marble entrance gate: "Colt Farm, Private Property, Public Welcome."

After his death in 1921 the farm survived several development scares until it was acquired by the State of Rhode Island through condemnation in 1965. Three years later it was dedicated as a state park.

The Walks

Four miles of paved paths snake around the property that opens up on the Narragansett Bay but your canine hiking here will likely be free form. Combine the bicycle paths with the expansive lawns and open spaces to carve out an outing with your dog. The open spaces are sprinkled with flowering fruit trees and trimmed bushes. This is easy, pleasant walking with your dog, almost always with a view of the bay.

Include a side trip over to the Bristol Town Beach to the north that allows dogs.

Trail Sense: There are no maps and no defined trailheads so just get out and start hiking.

> ### *Bonus*
> It was Samuel Colt's dream to breed the world's finest herd of Jersey cows. To that end he outfitted his massive stone barn with cork and rubber-covered flooring and thick beds of fresh straw. The barn was heated in the winter and the herd was attended to by a large staff with a ratio of one man for every five cows. The bulls' horns were polished and their tails washed every day. The prized herd travelled to county and state fairs around the country in specially padded railroad cars. At the entrance to Colt State Park this bovine legacy is remembered by bronze statues of two Jersey bulls, sculpted in France.
> The one on the right was one of Colt's favorites, a champion sire. The other was another champion brought to breed but soon after arriving in bristol killed a farm worker. The bull was destroyed and buried behind the stone barn.

Dog Friendliness
Dogs are welcome to join the fun in this popular park.

Traffic
Considered the gem of the Rhode Island state park system, Colt State Park is a crowded place with cyclists, joggers, picnickers and more.

Canine Swimming
Your dog can expect first-rate swimming here - at the very least your dog can swim in the Narragansett Bay at the boat ramp.

Trail Time
As much or as little as your dog desires.

19
Kettle Pond Visitor Center

Charlestown

Phone Number
- (401) 364-9124

Website
- www.friendsnwr-ri.org

Admission Fee
- None

Directions
- Kettle Pond is on the north side of Route 1, west of Charlestown.

The Park

Kettle Pond, the newest addition to the National Wildlife Refuge system in Rhode Island was acquired in 2001 and serves as the headquarters for the U.S. Fish & Wildlife Service in the state.

The land here was shaped by slow-moving glaciers churning across the landscape. The "ice bulldozer" carried giant boulders for hundreds of miles and scraped the ridges and depressions on this property that was once used for sheep farming.

The Walks

Kettle Pond features four marked trails, three of which are open to dogs. Most canine hikers will do two trails located on either side of the Visitor Center. The *Ocean View Trail* wiggles through pitch and white pines behind the Center to a high point with views south to Ninigret Pond and the open water. This linear trail is about a half-mile long.

From the parking lot the *Watchaug Trail* twists for a half-mile down to the namesake pond. This is easy canine hiking with gentle slopes and wide passages under the oaks and pines. Drifting off this path is the *Burlingame Trail* that leads to Burlingame State Park and longer hikes with your dog.

Trail Sense: There is a trailmap available at the trailhead by the parking lot.

Bonus
After you leave the trails take a look at the Visitor Center building, named a Federal Energy Saver Showcase for 2005. Building materials used for the project included durable and long-lived recycled materials with no or low-emissions, such as engineered wood, plastic lumber, linoleum flooring, fiberboard, sheetrock, tile, bamboo flooring, and carpet with high recycled content. Super insulation, energy-efficient lighting and windows, passive solar architecture, and a 40-ton renewable geothermal heat exchange system will help to save as much as 40 percent of traditional building energy costs.

Dog Friendliness
Dogs are not allowed on the *Toupoysett Trail*.
Traffic
Foot traffic only allowed on the trails.
Canine Swimming
Down at Watchaug Pond is super dog paddling.
Trail Time
About one hour.

20
Roger Williams Park

The Park

By the time of the American Civil War the city of Providence was becoming choked with development. You could walk block after block and never see a greenspace. In 1871 Betsey Williams bequeathed her 102-acre farm to the City of Providence for public use in memory of her ancestor, Roger Williams, who founded the city 235 years earlier after being banished from the Massachusetts Bay Colony.

The next year America's third zoo, a menagerie really, opened on the property. Today's zoo goers would probably have been disappointed with the rabbits and squirrels and raccoons and mice that were on display.

Soon the city annexed some land from adjacent Cranston and set out to build a first-rate urban park. They contacted Frederick Olmsted and Calvert Vaux, fathers of American landscape architecture, who both turned the job down, citing a need for more land. Horace Cleveland, a lesser contributor to the development of Central Park in New York and brother of President Grover Cleveland, did accept the assignment. He drained swamps to create clear water ponds and built stone bridges to connect islands and shaped the park seen today.

The Walks

If your idea of a canine hike is unbroken stretches of leafy solitude, this is not the place to come, as fine an example of an urban park as Roger Williams Park is. But there are walkways across rolling hills and long stretches around the park's many lakes to enjoy with your dog.

Providence

Phone Number
- (609) 861-2404

Website
- www.rogerwilliamsparkzoo.org

Admission Fee
- None

Directions
- From Interstate 95 South take Exit 17 onto Elmwood Avenue. Turn left at the ligt and make the second left into the park. From Interstate 95 North take Exit 16 and bear right. Turn left at the light and into the park on the right.

> ***Bonus***
> Make sure to take your dog for a walk around the Casino, built from a design by Providence architect Edwin T. Banning in 1890. Considered "The Jewel of Providence" the brick building is a classic example of Colonial Revival architecture. It was erected for $25,000 raised from boat rentals on the lakes in Roger Williams Park.

On the opposite sides of the lakes you can get off the pavement on narrow dirt ribbons. There are patches of forest but most of your dog's day will be spent in open air or isolated trees.

Trail Sense: A brochure is available that has a map of the major attractions in the park but there is no trail map.

Dog Friendliness
Dogs are allowed on the park grounds but not in the zoo.

Traffic
This is a very busy park with visitation measured in the millions but with a bit of hiking you can reach some peaceful areas in less developed sections of the park.

Canine Swimming
On some of the more remote places of the lakes your dog may be able to slip in for a dip.

Trail Time
Several hours.

21
Rhode Island Bikeways

The Park

Due to its compact size, Rhode Island is tailor-made for bike paths and greenways in the form of linear parks. Many of these trails have been developed in the corridors first created by railroads more than a century ago.

Railroads often built their roads on some of the most scenic landscape available to help lure riders and that makes many of these greenways especially attractive for recreation seekers today. Of course canine hikers are not the prime audience for these heavily used, narrow bands. Cyclists, inline skaters, rollerbladers, crosscountry skiers in winter - all can be a nuisance to an easily distracted dog. These are their paths and on crowded days you can most surely find easier places to hike with your dog. Still, their convenience and bucolic feel are often hard to resist.

Providence

Phone Number
- (401) 789-1706

Website
- www.rigreenways.org

Admission Fee
- None

Directions
- Varied

The Walks

Below are several bikeways you can try with your dog:

Blackstone River Bikeway

The plan here is to trace the old Blackstone Canal towpath built in 1828 from Providence north to Worcester, Massachusetts. The middle segment of over 7 leafy miles is complete along the lively Blackstone River with another dozen or so to come. There is parking for the trail in Blackstone State Park on Lower River road and off Route 116 near the George Washington Bridge-Lincoln side.

East Bay Bike Path

These 15 scrumptious miles from Providence to Bristol take in long looks of Upper Narragansett Bay and Providence Harbor, plus coastal marshes and ponds. This was once the route of the Providence, Warren & Bristol Railroad. Dedicated in 1992, the first complete bikeway in Rhode Island often sports a roomy shoulder that enables you to keep out of the wheeled traffic and provide a respite for the pounding of paw on asphalt. Jump on from Veteran's Memorial Parkway in East Providence or on Franklin Street in Warren.

South County Bicycle Path

This path will eventually stretch from the Narragansett Towers on the shore to the Great Swamp and the village of Peace Dale. Presently you can hike with your dog out in the western legs of the trail. Start your canine hike at the Kingston train Station off Route 138 in West Kingston.

Warwick & Cranston Bike Paths

Someday cyclists - and hardcore canine hikers - will be able to traverse the state from Providence to the Connecticut border on this abandoned railroad right-of-way. At present five of the 25 miles are ready to put paw to asphalt.

West Warwick & Coventry Bike Paths

Once trains on the Hartford, Providence & Fishkill Railroad chugged along this route connecting the two state capitals and eventually the Hudson River. Today canine hikers can use three miles of former railway in West Warwick from the town park on Hay Street near the Rhode Island Food Bank.

22
Snake Den State Park

The Park

Samuel Steere was the original settler of this land, back in 1786. As he and other farmers began clearing space for crops they leveled an area all around the series of bluffs and rocky ledges. The pioneers are thought to have described the crags as being covered with rattlesnakes, hence the genesis of the park's name (snakes still live in the area but reports of rattlesnakes are as rare as large tracts of open space like this is suburban Providence).

The Steere family worked the land for more than a century, prospering behind the yield of apple harvests and dairy operations. In 1890 James Dame bought the farm and met decidedly harder times. The Macintosh apple was introduced and quickly swamped the market. The Dame orchard had no Macintosh trees. When the Hurricane of 1938 came ashore the Dames barely had an orchard.

Eventually the farm was condemned by the state to be protected as a natural area. The Dame descendants were permitted to farm a portion of the parkland, continuing the tradition of over 200 years.

Johnston

Phone Number
- (401) 222-2632

Website
- www.riparks.com/snakeden.htm

Admission Fee
- None

Directions
- From Interstate 295 take Exit 6 onto Hartford Avenue. Head west for 1.5 miles to the third light and turn right. Go past Dame Farm and park in unmarked areas in the woods.

The Walks

The nearly 1000 acres of Snake Den State Park is undeveloped. It is hard to find signage or parking and dirt trails are unmarked and unmaintained. That sounds like a meat bone to a canine hiker. From the parking lot at the chained farm road on the edge of Dame Farm natural surface trails fan out towards the Snake Den. Up the hill to the left you can get a sense of the rocky terrrain that marks most of this natural area. Moving straight ahead on the farm road you

> *Bonus*
> The working Dame Farm provides a reminder of Rhode Island life from yesteryear - the small family farm selling produce locally.
> Several farm buildings, including the core of the farmhouse that is original back to 1786, have been placed on the National Register of Historic Places. The farm is open to the public seasonally.

soon reach an abandoned quarry and beyond that a stone wall where you will begin to encounter the granite crags.

This is easy hiking for your dog. The wooded terrain moves up and down but that only makes the walk interesting, not tiring.

Trail Sense: There are no navigation aids whatsoever but the route is straightforward.

Dog Friendliness
Dogs can explore the crags at the Snake Den.
Traffic
Most days you would be unlucky to run into another trail user.
Canine Swimming
Just a small stream runs through this area of the park.
Trail Time
An hour or more is possible in these woods.

23
Melville Ponds Recreation Area

The Park

This 152-acre property was controlled by the United States Navy from 1940 to 1978 who intended to use it as the Portsmouth Melville Dump. But groundwater from nearby wetlands scuttled that plan and nothing more than brush was ever disposed of here.

The property was deeded to the Town of Portsmouth by the U.S. Department of the Interior (DOI) in 1978 and is currently used a campground and recreational area.

The Walks

The canine hiking at Melville Ponds is packed into a thickly forested wedge hard by the Narragansett Bay. The marquee trail here is the *Blue Trail*

> **Portsmouth**
>
> Phone Number
> - None
>
> Website
> - None
>
> Admission Fee
> - None
>
> Directions
> - The park is north of Newport off Route 114. Turn west into the Melville Ponds Marina and make a right after .4 of a mile onto Sullivan Road at the sign for the campground. Continue to the end, make a left and a quick right to the parking lot before the trailhead.

that - after an unpromising beginning at a blocked chain fence - drops down to work its way along both sides of Lower Melville Pond. This is meant to be a one-mile loop but crossing at the top (across a series of waterfalls) and the bottom are a bit tricky, if not outright unpassable.

The *Orange Trail* is a loop that can get overgrown on narrow passages but provides access to a utility cut that leads across some railroad tracks (the Newport dinner train) and to the Narragansett Bay. You can use the Blue Trail and return along the dark and quiet Lower Melville Pond to create a hiking loop of a little less than two miles. An old water tower located off the Orange Trail is likely to get your dog's attention as you go past.

Trail Sense: The trails are blazed but trailmaps at the bulletin board would be a big help in exploring this property.

> **Bonus**
> Looking for a secluded fishing hole to work with your dog? The ponds here are stocked with game fish.

Dog Friendliness
Dogs are allowed on the Melville Pond trails and in the campground.
Traffic
Foot traffic only - and not a great deal of it.
Canine Swimming
There is plenty of good dog paddling in the Melville ponds and in the Narragansett Bay.
Trail Time
About one mile.

Dogs aren't the only ones to come to Melville Ponds for the quiet beauty.

24
Fort Getty Recreation Area

The Park
Just before the advent of the airplane that would revolutionize warfare the United States embarked on a widespread initiative to fortify the nation's coastal defenses. The War Department bought 31 acres on Conanicut Island and built Fort Getty, named for career military officer George Washington Getty. It was designed to defend Narragansett Bay's West Passage against invading fleets.

The fort was closed in 1943 and today the area is a popular summer campground on an exposed bluff above the bay.

The Walks
A park that is a little rough around the edges is a natural for dog owners - those pesky restrictions are liable to be a little more lax in such places - and Fort Getty fits the bill handsomely. Guided canine hiking is limited to the *Kit Wright Nature Trail* that trips along the west side of Fox Hill Salt Marsh for a short while.

In the off-season this is a great place for the dog to romp among the stacked picnic tables and open spaces.

Jamestown

Phone Number
- None

Website
- None

Admission Fee
- Yes, in summer

Directions
- From Route 138 exit towards the town of Jamestown on North Main Road. Continue to South East Avenue and pick up Beavertail Road. Fort Getty is on the right, just past Mackerel Cove.

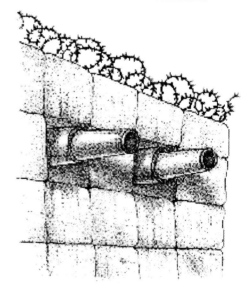

> **_Bonus_**
> From Fort Getty you can see the Dutch Island Light that was put into service in 1827 on a 30-foot tower built of stones found on the island.
> The first keeper was William Dennis, an American Revolution veteran who took the job att he age of 77. Dennis remained keeper until his death at 93.
> His son, Robert, later served as keeper.
> The Dutch Island Light lasted until 1979 when it was replaced by offshore buoys. Over the years preservation groups have worked to insure its survival but its future is still much in doubt.

Trail Sense: The Kit Wright Nature Trail is a one-way affair, marked on each end by a sign.

Dog Friendliness
Dogs are welcome in the park and in the campground.
Traffic
Almost none in the off-season.
Canine Swimming
A boat ramp extends down off the bluff into the bay for excellent access to the bay for your water-loving dog.
Trail Time
Less than one hour.

> *"He is very imprudent, a dog is. He never makes it his*
> *business to inquire whether you are in the right or in the wrong,*
> *never bothers as to whether you are going up or down upon life's ladder,*
> *never asks whether you are rich or poor, silly or wise,*
> *sinner or saint.""*
> *-Jerome K. Jerome*

25
Diamond Hill Park

The Park
Diamond Hill opened in the late 1930s as a hike-up-and-ski operation. There was a 1000-foot toboggan run and night skiing. Later additional ski trails were added and Ski Valley opened on the opposite side of the hill. Tow ropes were installed. The vertical drop reached as high as 300 feet over the next few decades and Diamond Hill is where hundreds of Rhode Islanders learned to ski on the "Big Hill."

The ski operation closed in the 1980s and Rhode Island managed the area as a state park. In 1997 ownership of the property was conveyed to the Town of Cumberland who built athletic fields and altered the feel of the park from passive to active.

Cumberland

Phone Number
- None

Website
- None

Admission Fee
- None

Directions
- The park is located in northeast Rhode Island, on Route 114, just south of the junction with Route 121.

The Walks
If you are looking for the steepest canine hike in Rhode Island - you've found it! The trail seems to go straight up and, covered in loose rocks, is even nastier coming down. Your dog's four-wheel drive is a definite asset on Diamond Hill. There are alternative routes to the top, remnants of the old ski runs, but you will no doubt want to test the hardest. Ten minutes of exertion should bring you to the summit.

If there are no games being played it is generally quiet enough in the park to poke around with your dog. One trip on Diamond Hill with its paw-grinding rocks will probably be enough. You may come across some trail marked by aluminum disks. This is the southern terminus of the *Warner Trail* that runs for 30 miles to Canton, Massachusetts. On May 19, 1951, Charlie Warner walked 25 miles on his trail when he was nearly 83 years of age. No word whether he had his dog with him.

> *Bonus*
> The views at the top of Diamond Hill will not cause you to sink to your knees in awe but it is a nice vista to the east over Pawtucket Reservoir.

Trail Sense: There are no maps and no trail markings that make any sense. Hopefully you will recognize Diamond Hill, accessed across a small stream.

Dog Friendliness
Dogs are allowed in Diamond Hill Park.
Traffic
You can ride a mountain bike up the Big Hill in theory but it is unlikely you will see any. The park gets light usage aside from ball games.
Canine Swimming
Silvy's Brook is a nice place to cool off but not deep enough for an extended swim.
Trail Time
An hour to completely explore the park, more if you set off towards Massachusetts on the Warner Trail.

It is a rocky road indeed to the top of Diamond Hill.

Taking Your Dog To The Roof Of Rhode Island

Highpointers are folks who seek to stand atop the highest point in each of the 50 states. The first person known to have tagged the summits of the 48 contiguous states was a fellow named Arthur Marshall back in 1936. After Hawaii and Alaska were added to the union in the 1950s, Vin Hoeman became the person to reach the top of all 50 states. To date fewer than 200 people have been documented to have climbed - as the case may be - all 50 highpoints.

Your dog can be a Highpointer too. She can't complete all the peaks - there are places she can't go legally (the spectacular Mount Katahdin at the northern terminus of the Appalachian Trail in Maine, for instance), mountains she can't climb physically (the vertical rock climbs at the top of Gannett Peak in Montana), or both (Mount McKinley, the highest of American peaks at over 20,000 feet). But that leaves plenty of state summits for your dog to experience.

The highest mountain in America's Lower 48 is California's Mount Whitney at 14,494 feet. But the hike to the top is not arduous and so popular permits are rationed out to get on the trail. You can hike with your dog to the shadow of the summit but the final steps will be yours alone as you leave the dog-friendly Inyo National Forest and travel into Sequoia National Park, where dogs are banned from the trails.

That leaves as the highest spot in America where your dog is allowed to go Mount Elbert in Colorado, only 61 feet lower than Whitney. Luckily, the hike to the top is again a relatively easy one and plenty of dogs make the day-trip every year. The round trip is between 9 and 15 miles, depending on how close to the trailhead your vehicle can get you, and there is no rock scrambling or "mountain climbing" necessary.

That is not the case with many of Mount Elbert's brethren in the West. The most accessible highpoints elsewhere over 10,000 feet are in the desert southwest. Wheeler Peak (13,161 feet) in New Mexico and Boundary Peak (13,143 feet) in Arizona are both conquerable by your dog.

Moving east, the jewel for Highpointers in the Great Plains is South Dakota's Harney Peak that lords over the Black Hills. At 7,242 feet, Harney is the highest point in America east of the Rocky Mountains. The canine ascent is steady but easily manageable for your dog,

with plenty of sitting room among the craggy rocks at the peak.

East of the Mississippi River there isn't a state high point your dog can't reach, save those on private or dog-restricted land. Of course, you don't need to climb at all on many - you can drive close to the top and take a short walk to the summit. Some of the famous auto mountain climbs are on Mount Washington (6,288 feet) in New Hamsphire , Mount Greylock (3,491 feet) in Massachusetts and Mount Mitchell (6,684 feet - the highest point east of the Mississippi) in North Carolina.

The smaller Eastern states also make it easier to tag several state highpoints on the same trip. In southwestern Pennsylvania your dog can make an easy one-mile hike to conquer Mount Davis (3,213 feet) then travel a few hours south to Backbone Mountain (3,360 feet) in Maryland. After you make the climb up an old fire road don't forget to sign the book with your dog's name and pick up a certificate validating his accomplishment. Next toodle over to Spruce Knob (4,863 feet) in West Virginia for a pleasant half-mile stroll from the parking lot atop the mountain to the actual summit.

So what about Rhode Island?

The highest point in the state is 812-foot Jerimoth Hill in Foster, on Hartford Road (Route 101), just west of the intersection with Route 94. For many years Jerimoth Hill was notorious as the most inaccessible high point in America, tougher to notch in a Highpointers' belt than even 20,320-foot Mount McKinley. Not for the difficult climb but because the highest piece of ground in Rhode Island is on private - often fiercely guarded - land.

Brown University owns the land of the actual high point (next to a rock, marked with an "X" on a tree) with the trail from the road to Jerimoth Hill passing through property of individual landowners. Highpointers Club members would return from an odyssey to Rhode Island with tales of verbal abuse, police reports and even encounters with the business end of a rifle.

The way to Jerimoth Hill has since changed hands and is more accessible today. There is a pleasant pine-straw trail (across the road from the sign marking Jerimoth Hill that is about 5 feet lower than the summit) of about 150 yards and your leashed dog is welcome to stand on the roof of Rhode Island.

But it is still private land and open on weekends only from 8:00 - 3:00. It is important to respect the privacy of the landowners and only come during these hours so Jerimoth Hill will remain open to all.

Your Dog At The Beach

It is hard to imagine many places a dog is happier than at a beach. Whether romping on the sand, digging a hole, jumping in the water or just lying in the sun, every dog deserves a day at the beach. But all too often dog owners stopping at a sandy stretch of beach are met with signs designed to make hearts - human and canine alike - droop: NO DOGS ON BEACH.

Rhode Island dogs are lucky dogs indeed. With some 400 miles of shoreline your wave-loving dog can enjoy a salt-water swim somewhere any time of the year - even in the summer. Below is a summary of rules for dogs at some of Rhode Island's many beaches...

Narragansett Bay

Barrington Town Beach
Barrington

No Dogs Allowed

Bristol Town Beach
Bristol

Dogs Allowed Year-Round

Conimicut Point Beach
Warwick

Dogs Allowed in off-season

Easton's Beach/First Beach
Newport

Dogs Allowed Labor Day-Memorial Day

Fogland Beach
Tiverton

Dogs Allowed Labor Day-Memorial Day

Fort Adams State Park
Newport

No Dogs Allowed

Goddard Memorial State Park Beach
Warwick

Dogs Allowed Labor Day-Memorial Day

Grinnell's Beach
Tiverton

Dogs Allowed Year-Round

King's Park
Newport

Dogs Allowed Year-Round

Mackerel Cove Jamestown	**Dogs Allowed Year-Round**
Oakland Beach Warwick	**Dogs Allowed Labor Day-Memorial Day**
Sandy Point Beach Portsmouth	**Dogs Allowed Year-Round**
Second Beach Middletown	**Dogs Allowed Labor Day-Memorial Day**
South Shore Beach Little Compton	**Dogs Allowed When Swimming Beach Is Closed**
Teddy's Beach Portsmouth	**Dogs Allowed Year-Round**
Warren Town Beach Warren	**No Dogs Allowed**

Atlantic Ocean

Ballard's Beach
Block Island

Dogs Allowed Year-Round

Black Rock Beach
Block Island

Dogs Allowed Year-Round

Blue Shutters Town Beach
Westerly

Dogs Allowed Labor Day-Memorial Day

Charlestown Town Beach
Charlestown

Dogs Allowed Labor Day-Memorial Day

Crescent Beach
Block Island

Dogs Allowed Year-Round

East Beach
Charlestown

Dogs Allowed October Through March

East Beach
Charlestown

Dogs Allowed October Through March

East Matunuck Beach
South Kingstown

Dogs Allowed October Through March

Misquamicut State Beach
Westerly

Dogs Allowed October Through March

Narragansett Town Beach
Narragansett

Dogs Allowed Labor Day-Memorial Day

Scarborough State Beach
Narragansett

Dogs Allowed Labor Day to First Saturday in May

South Kingstown Town Beach
Matunuck

Dogs Allowed October Through March

Watch Hill Beach
Watch Hill

Dogs Allowed Year-Round

Tips For Taking Your Dog To The Beach

- The majority of dogs can swim and love it, but dogs entering the water for the first time should be tested; never throw a dog into the water. Start in shallow water and call your dog's name - or try to coax him in with a treat or toy. Always keep your dog within reach.

- Another way to introduce your dog to the water is with a dog that already swims and is friendly with your dog. Let your dog follow his friend.

- If your dog begins to doggie paddle with his front legs only, lift his hind legs and help him float. He should quickly catch on and will keep his back end up.

- Swimming is a great form of exercise, but don't let your dog overdo it. He will be using new muscles and may tire quickly.

- Be careful of strong tides that are hazardous for even the best swimmers.

- Cool ocean water is tempting to your dog. Do not allow him to drink too much sea water. Salt in the water will make him sick. Salt and other minerals found in the ocean can damage your dog's coat so regular bathing is essential.

- Check with a lifeguard for daily water conditions - dogs are easy targets for jellyfish and sea lice.

- Dogs can get sunburned, especially short-haired dogs and ones with pink skin and white hair. Limit your dog's exposure when the sun is strong and apply sunblock to his ears and nose 30 minutes before going outside.

- If your dog is out of shape, don't encourage him to run on the sand, which is strenuous exercise and a dog that is out of shape can easily pull a tendon or ligament.

Dog-Friendly Campgrounds

Blackstone Valley

Bowdish Lake Camping Area (401) 568-8890
Glocester

Buck Hill Family Campground (401) 568-0456
Burrillville

Dyer Woods Nudist Campground (401) 397-3007
Foster

Ginny-B Family Campground (401) 397-9477
Foster

Holiday Acres Campground (401) 934-0780
Glocester

Oak Leaf Family Campground (401) 568-4446
Glocester

Whippoorwill Hill Family Campground (401) 397-7256
Foster

Newport County

Fort Getty Recreation Area (401) 423-7211
Jamestown

Meadowlark Recreational Vehicle Park (401) 846-9455
Middletown

South County

Breakwater Village Campground (401) 783-9527
Narragansett

Colwell's Campground (401) 397-4614
Coventry

Frontier Family Camper Park (401) 377-4510
Hopkinton

Greenwood Hill Campground (401) 539-7154
Hopkinton

Hickory Ridge Family Campground (401) 397-7474
Coventry

Long Cove Marina Family Campsites (401) 783-4902
Narragansett

Peeper Pond Campground (401) 294-5540
Glocester

Timber Creek RV Resort (401) 322-1877
Burrillville

Whispering Pines Campground (401) 539-7011
Hopkinton

Dog Parks

Dog parks often begin as informal gatherings of dog owners that eventaully become legitimized by local government. A dog park can be a place for your dog to run off-leash or romp with other dogs or a chance for you to play with your dog in a friendly environment. Here are some tips for enjoying your visit to the dog park:

- Keep an eye on your dog and a leash in hand. Situations can change quickly in a dog park.

- Keep puppies younger than 4 months at home until they have all necessary innoculations to allow them to play safely with other dogs. Make certain that your older dog is current on shots and has a valid license.

- ALWAYS clean up after your dog. Failure to pick up your dog's poop is the quickest way to spoil a dog park for every one.

- If your dog begins to play too rough, don't take time to sort out blame - leash the dog and leave immediately.

- Leave your female dog at home if she is in heat.

- Don't volunteer to bring all the dogs in the neighborhood with you when you go. Don't bring any more dogs than you can supervise comfortably.

- Observe and follow all posted regulations at the dog park.

- HAVE AS MUCH FUN AS YOUR DOG.

Bristol Paw Park *(Bristol: Colt Neck State Park, Route 114)*
An area has been set aside for off-leash play along the East Bay Bike Path.

Kimberly Perrott Memorial Paw Park *(Barrington: Route 103)*
This Barrington dog park carries the name of its greatest champion in ushering it into existence. Kimberly Perrott, a professional dog walker, passed away just months before the fenced park opened. The play area can be found behind the ballfields in the park, in the far western area.

Newport Dog Park *(Newport: JT Connell Highway at the foot of the Pell Bridge across from the Newport Playhouse)*
It's easy for your dog to miss the sea breezes in this fenced-in run squeezed into an industrial setting. No shade and wood chips play the role of grass for the most part.

Warwick Dog Park *(Warwick: Buttonwoods Park, Asylum Road)*
This pooch playground features 33,000 square feet of leg room with trees and grass. Surplus fire hydrants from the city's Public Works departments are a nice touch.

Index To Parks

	page
Arcadia Management Area	16
Beavertail State Park	22
Blackstone River Bikeway	56
Brenton Point State Park	38
Buck Hill Management Area	34
Burlingame State Park	42
Clay Head Nature Trail	24
Cliff Walk	28
Colt State Park	50
Cumberland Monastery	46
Diamond Hill Park	64
East Bay Bike Path	56
Fort Barton Nature Trail	40
Fort Wetherill	44
George Washington Management Area	26
Getty Recreation Area	62
Goddard Memorial State Park	18
The Greenway	20
Heritage Park	32
Kettle Pond Visitor Center	52
Lincoln Woods State Park	48
Melville Ponds	60
Prudence Island	36
Roger Williams Park	54
Snake Den State Park	58
South County Bicycle Path	56
Warwick & Cranston Bike Path	56
Weetamoo Woods	30
West Warwick & Coventry Bike Paths	56

As a young lawyer, 19th century Senator George Graham Vest of Missouri, addressed the jury on behalf of his client, suing a neighbor who had killed his dog. Vest's speech has come to be known as "Tribute to the Dog."

The best friend a man has in the world may turn against him and become his enemy. His son or daughter that he has reared with loving care may prove ungrateful. Those who are nearest and dearest to us, those whom we trust with our happiness and our good name may become traitors to their faith. The money that a man has, he may lose. It flies away from him, perhaps when he needs it most. A man's reputation may be sacrificed in a moment of ill-considered action. The people who are prone to fall on their knees to do us honor when success is with us may be the first to throw the stone of malice when failure settles its cloud upon our heads. The one absolutely unselfish friend that man can have in this selfish world, the one that never deserts him, the one that never proves ungrateful or treacherous is his dog. A man's dog stands by him in prosperity and in poverty, in health and in sickness. He will sleep on the cold ground, where the wintry winds blow and the snow drives fiercely, if only he may be near his master's side. He will kiss the hand that has no food to offer; he will lick the wounds and sores that come in an encounter with the roughness of the world. He guards the sleep of his pauper master as if he were a prince. When all other friends desert, he remains. When riches take wings, and reputation falls to pieces, he is as constant in his love as the sun in its journey through the heavens. If fortune drives the master forth an outcast in the world, friendless and homeless, the faithful dog asks no higher privilege than that of accompanying him, to guard him against danger, to fight against his enemies. And when the last scene of all comes, and death takes his master in its embrace and his body is laid away in the cold ground, no matter if all other friends pursue their way, there by the graveside will the noble dog be found, his head between his paws, his eyes sad, but open in alert watchfulness, faithful and true even in death.

Other Canine Hiking Books From Cruden Bay Books

The Canine Hiker's Bible: A Companion For The Active Dog Owner

Doggin' Delaware: The 40 Best Places to Hike With Your Dog In The Diamond State

Doggin' Jersey: The 100 Best Places to Hike With Your Dog In The Garden State

Doggin' Maryland: The 100 Best Places to Hike With Your Dog In The Free State

Doggin' Northern Virginia: The 50 Best Places to Hike With Your Dog In The Old Dominion

Doggin' Connecticut: The 100 Best Places to Hike With Your Dog In The Nutmeg State

A Bark In The Park: The 55 Best Places To Hike With Your Dog In The Philadelphia Region

A Bark In The Park: The 50 Best Places To Hike With Your Dog In The Baltimore Region

A Bark In The Park: The 44 Best Places To Hike With Your Dog In The Cincinnati Region

A Bark In The Park: The 45 Best Places To Hike With Your Dog In The Portland, Oregon Region

A Bark In The Park: The 40 Best Places To Hike With Your Dog In The Reno/Lake Tahoe Region

A Bark In The Park: The 48 Best Places To Hike With Your Dog In The Black Hills

Printed in the United States
117832LV00003B/112-135/A